```
MW01490112
```

Johann Wolfgang von Goethe: A Short Biography

Johann Wolfgang von Goethe, one of the most prominent figures in German literature, was born on August 28, 1749, in Frankfurt am Main, in the Holy Roman Empire. He was the eldest of seven children in a prosperous family, of which only he and his sister survived. His father, Johann Caspar Goethe, was a lawyer and his mother, Catharina Elisabeth Goethe, came from a wealthy family. This privileged background provided Goethe with a solid foundation for his future pursuits.

Goethe's early years were marked by a strong interest in literature and the arts. He was a precocious child, and his love for reading and writing was evident from a young age. He was educated at home by private tutors and displayed an exceptional aptitude for languages, learning French, Italian, English, and Latin alongside his native German.

In 1765, at the age of 16, Goethe began studying law at the University of Leipzig, as per his father's wishes. However, his heart was more drawn to literature and the arts than to legal studies. During his time at Leipzig, he became involved in the local literary scene and met important figures who would influence his future work.

Goethe's true breakthrough came when he transferred to the University of Strasbourg in

1770 to pursue a law degree. It was during this period that he encountered the works of Enlightenment thinkers such as Voltaire and Rousseau, which significantly shaped his intellectual development. He also immersed himself in the world of poetry, joining literary circles and becoming friends with the poet Johann Gottfried Herder.

In October 1770, Goethe's life took a pivotal turn when he fell in love with Friederike Brion, the daughter of a pastor in the village of Sesenheim. This passionate and tumultuous love affair would inspire some of his most famous works, including "The Sorrows of Young Werther," a novel that would catapult him to literary fame.

After completing his studies in Strasbourg, Goethe returned to Frankfurt in 1771 and briefly worked as a lawyer. However, his heart remained dedicated to literature and the arts. In 1774, Goethe produced one of his most famous creations, "The Sorrows of Young Werther," a semi-autobiographical tale of unrequited love that became a sensation across Europe. The novel's romanticism and emotional depth resonated with readers and established Goethe as a leading figure of the Sturm und Drang (Storm and Stress) literary movement. His growing reputation as a poet led to his appointment as a member of the Duke of Saxe-Weimar's court in 1775.

Artistic and Scientific Pursuits in Weimar

Goethe's relocation to Weimar marked a turning point in his life, setting the stage for a remarkable period of literary and intellectual growth. During this phase, he created some of his most enduring works and solidified his status as one of the most influential figures in the history of German literature.

Among these works was the publication of 'Faust' in 1808, a masterful epic that delves into the complex journey of its protagonist, Heinrich Faust, on a relentless quest for knowledge, pleasure, and purpose. Although incomplete during his lifetime, this masterpiece is considered one of the greatest achievements in world literature, exploring the timeless struggle between good and evil through the character of Faust, a man who makes a pact with the devil.

Goethe's interests were not confined to literature and the arts. He made significant contributions to various fields, including natural science. His observations of color theory and plant morphology, as detailed in his work "Theory of Colours" and "Metamorphosis of Plants," influenced later scientists and thinkers.

Goethe's position at the Weimar court allowed him to interact with a wide range of intellectuals and artists. He formed a deep and lasting friendship with the playwright and philosopher Friedrich Schiller. Their collaboration and intellectual exchange gave rise to some of their most celebrated works. The most notable of these is the "Weimar Classicism," a literary movement that sought to blend classical and romantic elements.

Goethe continued to write prolifically throughout his life, producing influential works like "Wilhelm Meister's Apprenticeship" and "Wilhelm Meister's Journeyman Years." He also worked on the second part of his magnum opus, 'Faust,' until his death, which was posthumously published.

Johann Wolfgang von Goethe passed away on March 22, 1832, in Weimar. His contributions to literature, science, and philosophy continue to be celebrated and studied worldwide. His works, particularly "The Sorrows of Young Werther," "Wilhelm Meister," and "Faust," have left an indelible mark on German literature and Western thought.

Goethe's exploration of human nature, the human condition, and the pursuit of knowledge and self-discovery in his writings have made him a timeless figure whose influence transcends borders and generations. His emphasis on the importance of individuality and self-expression has inspired countless artists and thinkers, ensuring that his legacy endures to this day.

A Look at Major Works by Goethe

1. Faust (Part 1 and Part 2):

"Faust" is one of Goethe's most significant and enduring works. It is a dramatic poem that tells the story of a man named Heinrich Faust, a scholar who is dissatisfied with his life and makes a pact with the devil, Mephistopheles, in exchange for knowledge, worldly pleasures, and ultimate fulfillment.

Part 1 of "Faust" primarily deals with Faust's dissatisfaction with his life and his desire to attain knowledge and worldly pleasure. He becomes involved with Mephistopheles, who leads him on a series of adventures and temptations. Faust falls in love with a young woman named Gretchen (or Margarete), and his actions lead to her tragic downfall.

Part 2 of "Faust" is a more complex and philosophical continuation of the story. Faust seeks to fulfill his ambition by engaging in political and economic endeavors, including draining a swamp to reclaim land. He aspires to achieve the ideal society. The work explores themes of human striving, redemption, and the Faustian pact in a broader sense.

"Faust" is renowned for its profound exploration of the human condition, the pursuit of knowledge and power, and the consequences of one's actions. It is considered a masterpiece of German literature and is often regarded as a symbol of the Faustian archetype, which represents humanity's unending desire for more.

2. The Sorrows of Young Werther:

"The Sorrows of Young Werther" is an epistolary novel by Goethe, published in 1774. It is considered one of the earliest examples of the Sturm und Drang (Storm and Stress) literary movement, which emphasized intense emotional expression and individualism.

The novel is presented as a series of letters written by the young protagonist, Werther, to his friend Wilhelm. Werther is a sensitive and passionate young man who moves to a small town and falls deeply in love with Charlotte (or Lotte), who is already engaged to another man. His unrequited love and emotional turmoil lead to a tragic and obsessive infatuation, ultimately culminating in his own suicide.

"The Sorrows of Young Werther" is notable for its emotional intensity and exploration of the young protagonist's inner struggles, as well as the theme of unfulfilled love. It had a significant influence on European Romantic literature and culture and was both celebrated and criticized for its portrayal of extreme emotions and its potential to inspire copycat suicides.

3. Wilhelm Meister's Apprenticeship (Wilhelm Meisters Lehrjahre):

"Wilhelm Meister's Apprenticeship" is a novel by Goethe, first published in 1795. It is often considered one of the earliest novels of the Bildungsroman genre, which focuses on the development and education of a young protagonist.

The story follows the life and adventures of Wilhelm Meister, a young man who embarks on a journey of self-discovery and personal growth. He starts as an actor but later explores other career paths and social milieus, including the world of theater, literature, and the aristocracy. Throughout the novel, Wilhelm seeks his true purpose in life, learns from his experiences, and matures as an individual.

The novel explores themes of self-realization, artistic ambition, and the search for identity. It also addresses the role of art and creativity in personal development. "Wilhelm Meister's Apprenticeship" is considered a significant work in the development of the German novel and Goethe's exploration of the human journey toward self-fulfillment.

4. Iphigenia in Tauris (Iphigenie auf Tauris):

"Iphigenia in Tauris" is a dramatic work by Goethe, based on the classical Greek myth of Iphigenia, the daughter of Agamemnon. It was first published in 1787 and is one of Goethe's classical dramas.

In the play, Iphigenia has been transported to the land of Tauris, where she serves as a priestess in a temple. The story revolves around themes of fate, familial bonds, and redemption. Iphigenia's character grapples with her past traumas and her longing for reunion with her family. The drama explores the conflict between duty and personal desires.

"Iphigenia in Tauris" is noted for its classical style and exploration of the complexities of human emotions and moral dilemmas. It remains a significant work in the tradition of classical drama with a Romantic sensibility.

5. Egmont:

"Egmont" is a tragedy written by Goethe and first published in 1788. The play is set in 16th-century Flanders and centers around the historical figure of Count Egmont, a nobleman who becomes a symbol of resistance against Spanish oppression.

The story portrays Egmont's efforts to defend the rights and liberties of the people of Flanders against the tyrannical rule of the Duke of Alba, representing Spanish authority. The play explores themes of freedom, political resistance, and the conflict between individual heroism and the demands of a repressive state.

"Egmont" is known for its eloquent language, and it became a symbol of national resistance and the fight for liberty in the face of oppression. It's often regarded as a classic of German literature and a reflection of Goethe's political and social concerns of his time.

6. Theory of Colours (Zur Farbenlehre):

"Theory of Colours" is a scientific and philosophical work by Goethe, published in 1810. In this work, Goethe explores the nature of colors and their perception. He rejected the prevailing Newtonian theory of colors and instead proposed his own theory, emphasizing the subjective and psychological aspects of color perception. Goethe's work had a significant impact on the development of color theory and is considered a precursor to modern color psychology.

7. The Metamorphosis of Plants (Versuch die Metamorphose der Pflanzen zu erklären):

"The Metamorphosis of Plants" is a botanical work by Goethe, published in 1790. In this essay,

Goethe presents his idea that all plant structures are derived from a basic form, which he called the "Urplanze" (primitive plant). He argued that the diverse parts of plants (leaves, flowers, etc.) were transformations of this basic plant form. This work was an early contribution to the study of plant morphology and the concept of the archetype in nature.

These two works, "Theory of Colours" and "The Metamorphosis of Plants," reflect Goethe's interests in scientific inquiry and the natural world, showcasing his multidisciplinary talents as a writer and thinker.

Goethe's Philosophy and the scope of this book

Goethe's philosophy encompasses several key ideas, including his emphasis on the interconnectedness of all aspects of life and his rejection of reductionist thinking. He believed in the organic unity of the world and saw nature, art, and human existence as integrated components of a holistic whole. Goethe also explored the duality of nature and human experience, embracing the coexistence of opposing elements in the world. In literature and philosophy, Goethe's exploration of archetypal patterns and universal human experiences influenced the development of Romanticism and Symbolism.
His multidisciplinary approach and dedication to a lifelong quest for knowledge and self-discovery continue to serve as a wellspring of inspiration for thinkers across various domains. This book of Goethe's quotes offers readers an insightful glimpse into his profound ideas.

One ought, every day at
least, to hear a little
song, read a good poem,
see a fine picture, and,
if it were possible,
to speak a few
reasonable words.

Our destiny often looks like a fruit-tree in winter. Who would think from its pitiable aspect that those rigid boughs, those rough twigs could next spring again be green, bloom, and even bear fruit? Yet we hope it, we know it.

The world is so empty
if one thinks only of
mountains, rivers
and cities; but to
know someone who
thinks and feels
with us, and who,
though distant, is
close to us in spirit,
this makes the earth
for us an inhabited
garden.

Our passions are
true phoenixes;
as the old burn out
the new straight
rise up from
the ashes.

If there is confusion
in your head and in
your heart, what more
do you want! A man
who no longer loves
and no longer errs
should have himself
buried straight away.

Take life too
seriously, and what
is it worth? If the
morning wake us to
no new joys, if the
evening bring us
not the hope of new
pleasure, is it
worthwhile to
dress and
undress?

Happy is it, indeed, for me that my heart is capable of feeling the same simple and innocent pleasure as the peasant whose table is covered with food of his own rearing, and who not only enjoys his meal, but remembers with delight the happy days and sunny mornings when he planted it, the soft evenings when he watered it, and the pleasure he experienced in watching its daily growth.

How many kings are governed by their ministers, how many ministers by their secretaries? Who, in such cases, is really the chief?

Talents are nurtured
best in solitude,
But character on life's
tempestuous seas!

Love does not
dominate,
it cultivates.
And that is more.

No two men see the world exactly alike, and different temperaments will apply in different ways a principle that they both acknowledge. The same man will, indeed, often see and judge the same things differently on different occasions: early convictions must give way to more mature ones. Nevertheless, may not the opinions that a man holds and expresses withstand all trials, if he only remains true to himself and others?

Seize this very
minute. What you can
do or dream you can
do, begin it. Begin it
and the work will be
completed.

All truly wise
thoughts have been
thought already
thousands of times;
but to make them
truly ours, we must
think them over again
honestly, till they
take firm root in our
personal experience.

It's true that
nothing in this
world makes us so
necessary to others
as the affection we
have for them.

He who has a task to
perform must know
how to take sides,
or he is quite
unworthy of it.

To live in a great idea
means to treat the
impossible as though
it were possible.
It is just the same
with a strong
character;
and when an idea and a
character meet, things
arise which fill the
world with wonder for
thousands of years.

Life belongs to
the living, and he
who lives must be
prepared for
changes.

Nothing shows a
man's character
more than what
he laughs at.

Whoever wishes to deny
nature as an organ of
the divine must begin
by denying all
revelation.

The world is for thousands
a freak show; the images
flicker past and vanish;
the impressions remain
flat and unconnected in
the soul. Thus they are
easily led by the opinions
of others, are content to
let their impressions be
shuffled and rearranged
and evaluated differently.

Beloved, don't fret that you
gave yourself so quickly!
Believe me, I don't think
badly or wrongly of you.
The arrows of Love are
various: some scratch us,
And our hearts suffer
for years from their
slow poison.
But others strong-
feathered with freshly
sharpened points
Pierce to the marrow, and
quickly inflame the blood.
In the heroic ages, when
gods and goddesses loved,
Desire followed a look,
and joy followed desire.

Art is in itself
noble; that is why the
artist has no fear of
what is common. This,
indeed, is already
ennobled when he
takes it up.

The human race is a
monotonous affair.
Most people spend the
greatest part of their
time working in order
to live, and what
little freedom remains
so fills them with fear
that they seek out any
and every means to be
rid of it.

All poetry is supposed to be instructive but in an unnoticeable manner; it is supposed to make us aware of what it would be valuable to instruct ourselves in; we must deduce the lesson on our own, just as with life.

When we take people
merely as they are,
we make them worse;
when we treat them
as if they were what
they should be, we
improve them as far
as they can be
improved.

He who is and remains
true to himself and to
others has the most
attractive quality of
the greatest talent.

It is difficult to
know how to treat the
errors of the age. If a
man oppose them, he
stands alone; if he
surrender to them,
they bring him
neither joy nor
credit.

Everything that frees our spirit without giving us control of ourselves is ruinous.

The highest goal that man can achieve is amazement.

Each has his own
happiness in his hands,
as the artist handles
the rude clay he seeks
to reshape it into a
figure; yet it is the
same with this art as
with all others: only
the capacity for it is
innate; the art itself
must be learned and
painstakingly
practiced.

Certain defects
are necessary for
the existence of
individuality.

Age does not
make us childish,
as men tell,
it merely finds us
children still at
heart.

Yes! to this thought
I hold with firm
persistence;
The last result of
wisdom stamps it true;
He only earns his
freedom and existence
Who daily conquers
them anew.

You ask which form
of government is
the best?
Whichever
teaches us to
govern ourselves.

He is happiest, be
he king or peasant,
who finds peace
in his home.

Life seems so vulgar, so easily content with the commonplace things of every day, and yet it always nurses and cherishes certain higher claims in secret, and looks about for the means of satisfying them.

A man sees in the
world what he
carries in his
heart.

I love those who
yearn for the
impossible.

As soon as you trust
yourself, you will
know how to live.

No one would talk
much in society,
if he knew how often
he misunderstands
others.

I examine my own being, and find there a world, but a world rather of imagination and dim desires, than of distinctness and living power. Then everything swims before my senses, and I smile and dream while pursuing my way through the world.

Behavior is the
mirror in which
everyone shows
their image.

If I love you,
what business is it
of yours?

Since Time is not a person we can overtake when he is gone, let us honor him with mirth and cheerfulness of heart while he is passing.

Mannerism is always longing to have done, and has no true enjoyment in work. A genuine, really great talent, on the other hand, has its greatest happiness in execution.

Beauty is a primeval phenomenon, which itself never makes its appearance, but the reflection of which is visible in a thousand different utterances of the creative mind, and is as various as nature herself.

With the growth of knowledge our ideas must from time to time be organized afresh. The change takes place usually in accordance with new maxims as they arise, but it always remains provisional.

In happy ignorance,
I sighed for a world I
did not know, where I
hoped to find every
pleasure and enjoyment
which my heart could
desire; and now, on my
return from that wide
world... how many
disappointed hopes and
unsuccessful plans
have I brought back!

None are so
hopelessly enslaved,
as those who falsely
believe they are free.
The truth has been
kept from the depth
of their minds by
masters who rule them
with lies. They feed
them on falsehoods
till wrong looks like
right in their eyes.

Nothing puts me so
completely out of
patience as the
utterance of a
wretched
commonplace
when I am talking
from my inmost heart.

And what does really
matter? That is easy:
thinking and doing,
doing and thinking—
and these are the sum
of all wisdom....
Both must move ever
onward in life, to and
fro, like breathing
in and breathing out.

When Nature begins to reveal her open secret to a man, he feels an irresistible longing for her worthiest interpreter, Art.

The artist has a twofold
relation to nature;
he is at once her master
and her slave. He is her
slave in that he must
work with ordinary
means, so as to be
understood, but her
master in that he
subjects these ordinary
means to his higher
purpose, making them
subservient to them.

The first look at the world, by the mind's eye, as well as by the bodily organs of vision, conveys no distinct impression, either to our heads or to our hearts. We see things without perceiving them, and it takes a long time before we learn to understand the things we see.

If one has not read the
newspapers for some
months and then reads
them all together, one
sees, as one never saw
before, how much time
is wasted with this
kind of literature.

There are three classes of readers; some enjoy without judgment; others judge without enjoyment; and some there are who judge while they enjoy, and enjoy while they judge. The latter class reproduces the work of art on which it is engaged. Its numbers are very small.

Only mankind
Can do the
impossible:
He can distinguish,
He chooses
and judges,
He can give
permanence
To the moment.

Every man bears
something within
him that, if it were
publicly announced,
would excite
feelings of
aversion.

In nature we never
see anything
isolated, but
everything in
connection with
something else
which is before it,
beside it, under it
and over it.

A human being needs
only a small plot of
ground on which to be
happy, and even less
to lie beneath.

The universe is a
harmonious whole,
each creature is
but a note, a shade
of a great harmony,
which man must
study in its
entirety and
greatness, lest
each detail should
remain a dead
letter.

Assuredly there is no more lovely worship of God than that for which no image is required, but which springs up in our breast spontaneously when nature speaks to the soul, and the soul speaks to nature face to face.

Correction does much,
but encouragement
does more.
Encouragement after
censure is as the sun
after a shower.

People are always talking about originality; but what do they mean? As soon as we are born, the world begins to work upon us; and this goes on to the end. And after all, what can we call our own, except energy, strength, and will? If I could give an account of all that I owe to great predecessors and contemporaries, there would be but a small balance in my favor.

Whatever is the
lot of humankind
I want to taste within
my deepest self.
I want to seize the
highest and the lowest,
to load its woe and
bliss upon my breast,
and thus expand my
single self titanically
and in the end go down
with all the rest.

Mere communion with nature, mere contact with the free air, exercise a soothing yet strengthening influence on the wearied spirit, calm the storm of passion, and soften the heart when shaken by sorrow to its inmost depths.

As for solitude, I cannot understand how certain people seek to lay claim to intellectual stature, nobility of soul and strength of character, yet have not the slightest feeling for seclusion; for solitude, I maintain, when joined with a quiet contemplation of nature, a serene and conscious faith in creation and the Creator, and a few vexations from outside is the only school for a mind of lofty endowment.

I reverence the
individual who
understands distinctly
what he wishes; who
unweariedly advances,
who knows the means
conducive to his
object, and can seize
and use them.

I nothing had, and yet
enough for youth—Joy
in Illusion, ardent
thirst for Truth. Give
unrestrained, the old
emotion, The bliss
that touched the verge
of pain, The strength
of Hate, Love's deep
devotion,—O, give me
back my youth again!

Courage and modesty are the most unequivocal of virtues, for they are of a kind that hypocrisy cannot imitate; they too have this quality in common, that they are expressed by the same color....

The written word has
this advantage, that
it lasts and can await
the time when it is
allowed to take
effect.

It is not always
needful for truth to
take a definite shape;
it is enough if it
hovers about us like a
spirit and produces
harmony; if it is
wafted through the air
like the sound of a
bell, grave and kindly.

Error is related to
truth as sleeping is
to waking. I have
observed that when
one has been in error,
one turns to truth as
though revitalized.

Nothing is more odious than the majority, for it consists of a few powerful leaders, a certain number of accommodating scoundrels and submissive weaklings, and a mass of men who trot after them without thinking, or knowing their own minds.

It used to happen, and still happens, to me to take no pleasure in a work of art at the first sight of it, because it is too much for me; but if I suspect any merit in it, I try to get at it; and then I never fail to make the most gratifying discoveries--to find new qualities in the work itself and new faculties in myself.

It is better to do
the smallest thing
in the world than to
hold half an hour to
be too small a thing.

Who is the happiest of men? He who values the merits of others, And in their pleasure takes joy, even as though 'twere his own. Not in the morning alone, not only at mid-day he charmeth; Even at setting, the sun is still the same glorious planet.

I'm sorry for people who make a great to-do about the transitory nature of things and get lost in meditations of earthly nothingness. Surely we are here precisely so as to turn what passes into something that endures; but this is possible only if you can appreciate both.

There is no outward mark of politeness that does not have a profound moral reason. The right education would be that which taught the outward mark and the moral reason together.

The world runs on
from one folly to
another; and the man
who, solely from
regard to the opinion
of others, and without
any wish or necessity
of his own, toils after
gold, honour, or any
other phantom, is no
better than a fool.

Flowers are
the beautiful
hieroglyphics of
nature with which
she indicates how
much she loves us.

We often feel that we lack something, and seem to see that very quality in someone else, promptly attributing all our own qualities to him too, and a kind of ideal contentment as well. And so the happy mortal is a model of complete perfection--which we have ourselves created.

He alone is great
and happy who fills
his own station of
independence, and
has neither to
command nor
to obey.

Everyone believes
in his youth that
the world really
began with him,
and that all merely
exists for his sake.

The highest
happiness of man ...
is to have probed
what is knowable
and quietly to
revere what is
unknowable.

A crisis must necessarily arise when a field of knowledge matures enough to become a science, for those who focus on details and treat them as separate will be set against those who have their eye on the universal and try to fit the particular into it.

I have found a paper
of mine among some
others in which I
call architecture
'petrified music.'
Really there is
something in this;
the tone of mind
produced by
architecture
approaches the
effect of music.

Sound and sufficient
reason falls, after
all, to the share of
but few men, and those
few men exert their
influence in silence.

A teacher who can
arouse a feeling for
one single good action,
for one single good
poem, accomplishes
more than he who fills
our memory with rows
on rows of natural
objects, classified
with name and form.

Sweet moonlight, shining
full and clear, Why do you
light my torture here?
How often have you seen me
toil, Burning last drops
of midnight oil. On books
and papers as I read,
My friend, your mournful
light you shed. If only I
could flee this den And
walk the mountain-tops
again, Through moonlit
meadows make my way,
In mountain caves with
spirits play – Released
from learning's musty
cell, Your healing dew
would make me well!

The architect hands over to the rich man with the keys to his palace all the ease and comfort to be found in it without being able to enjoy any of it himself. Must the artist not in this way gradually become alienated from his art, since his work, like a child that has been provided for and left home, can no longer have any effect upon its father? And how beneficial it must have been for art when it was intended to be concerned almost exclusively with what was public property, and belonged to everybody and therefore also to the artist!

Men who give way
easily to tears are
good. I have nothing
to do with those who
hearts are dry and
who eyes are dry!

An old foundation is
worthy of all respect,
but it must not take
from us the right to
build afresh
wherever
we will.

I am proud of my heart
alone, it is the sole
source of everything,
all our strength,
happiness and misery.
All the knowledge I
possess everyone else
can acquire, but my
heart is all my own.

Everything that we call Invention or Discovery in the higher sense of the word is the serious exercise and activity of an original feeling for truth, which, after a long course of silent cultivation, suddenly flashes out into fruitful knowledge.

I could never have known so well how paltry men are, and how little they care for really high aims, if I had not tested them by my scientific researches. Thus I saw that most men only care for science so far as they get a living by it, and that they worship even error when it affords them a subsistence.

Words are good, but
there is something
better. The best cannot
be explained by words.
The spirit in which we
act is the chief matter.
Action can only be only
understood and
represented
by the spirit.

You often say to yourself in the course of your life that you ought to avoid having too much business, 'polypragmosyne' [incessant activity], and, more especially, that the older you get, the more you ought to avoid entering on new business. But it's all very well saying this, and giving yourself and others good advice. The very fact of growing older means taking up a new business; all our circumstances change, and we must either stop doing anything at all or else willing and consciously take on the new role we have to play on life's stage.

What wise or
stupid thing
can man conceive
That was not
thought of in
ages long ago?

The first and last
thing demanded of
genius is love of
truth.

Poetry is the
universal
possession of
mankind, revealing
itself everywhere,
and at all times,
in hundreds and
hundreds of men.

Nothing venture,
nothing gain.
Who ne'er his bread
in sorrow ate,
Who ne'er the mournful
midnight hours
Weeping upon his bed
has sate,
He knows you not, ye
Heavenly Powers.

Divide and rule, the
politician cries;
unite and lead, is
watchword of the
wise.

Is this the destiny of man? Is he only happy before he has acquired his reason or after he has lost it?

When young, one is
confident to be able
to build palaces for
mankind, but when
the time comes one
has one's hands full
just to be able to
remove their trash.

We are so
constituted that
we believe the most
incredible things;
and, once they are
engraved upon the
memory, woe to him
who would endeavor
to erase them.

Haste not!
Rest not!
Calmly wait;
Meekly bear the
storms of fate!
Duty be thy
polar guide,—
Do the right,
whate'er betide!
Haste not! Rest not!
Conflicts past,
God shall crown
thy work at last.

Made in United States
Troutdale, OR
09/16/2024

22880105R00072